# WOOD

Sue Dyson

Thomson Learning
New York

## Books in this series

| | |
|---|---|
| Bricks | Paper |
| Electricity | Plastics |
| Gas | Steel |
| Glass | Water |
| Oil | Wood |

**Cover:** (Main picture) Builders nailing cedar boards onto a house in Massachusetts. (Top right) Wooden logs.

First published in the
United States in 1993 by
Thomson Learning
115 Fifth Avenue
New York, NY 10003

First published in 1991 by
Wayland (Publishers) Ltd

Cataloging-in-Publication Data applied for

ISBN: 1-56847-043-6

Printed in Italy

# Contents

All the words that appear in
**bold** are explained in the
glossary on page 30.

# What is wood?

Wood is used by people all over the world. It is one of the most important materials we have. It can be used for many different things. Boats, paper, furniture, and houses are just some of the things that can be made from wood. Wood is strong, springy, warm to the touch, and can be cut into any shape. If it is well taken care of, wood can last for hundreds of years.

*A map of the world showing where most of the hardwood and softwood trees grow.*

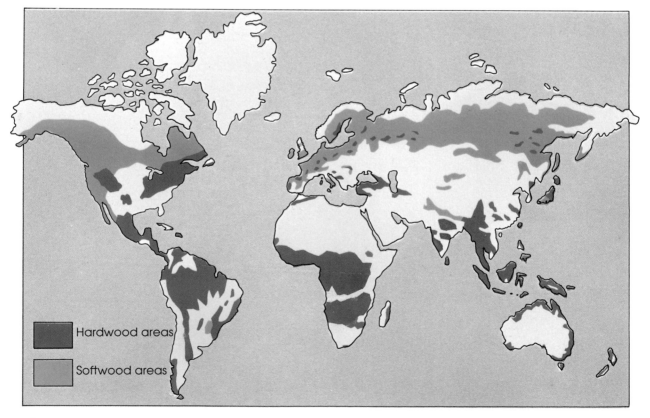

Hardwood areas

Softwood areas

Wood comes from the trunks and branches of trees. Different trees give us different kinds of wood. There are two main types of trees, **softwoods** and **hardwoods**. But this does not mean that their wood is either hard or soft. Softwood trees have thin, needlelike leaves and carry their seeds in cones. They grow best in countries that have cold, dry **climates**.

Hardwood trees have broad leaves and grow best in countries that have mild climates or in hot, wet places like **tropical rain forests**. Most hardwood trees are deciduous, which means they lose their leaves each autumn.

*In the autumn, a Japanese forest shows a mixture of hardwood and softwood trees.*

5

# Growing trees for wood

Around one-third of the earth's land is covered by forests. But many forests are being cut down to clear land for farming. And many of the trees in these forests are not being replaced by planting new trees.

Foresters plan and plant forests to provide a steady supply of wood. This means that when trees are cut down, new ones are planted to take their place.

*A forester plants young saplings.*

*Saplings grown from seed in a Brazilian nursery.*

Foresters grow the trees from seed in **nurseries**. When the young trees are big enough, they are planted outside. After four years, the **saplings** are replanted in the forest or plantation. Both softwood and hardwood trees are grown in plantations. Hardwoods take longer to grow than softwoods.

*The number of growth rings on a tree stump shows the age of the tree.*

Each spring, trees grow a new layer of wood. If you look at a tree stump, you will see lots of rings, one inside the other. These rings show each year's new growth. You can count the rings to find out how old the tree is.

# Harvesting the forests

When the trees in the plantation are big enough, they are harvested by loggers who use chain saws. This is very skilled work. The trees must fall in the right place and must not damage the trees around them.

Once the trees have been **felled**, their branches are cut off. This makes them easier to transport. The logs are stacked in piles and are loaded by machine onto trucks or trains to go to a **sawmill**. In some countries, the logs are floated down a river to the sawmill. On steep slopes, helicopters may be used to drag the logs away.

**Above** *A logger felling a tree with a chain saw.*

**Below** *These heavy logs are being transported by truck and train.*

Foresters make sure that the right number of trees are harvested. In tropical rain forests, there are no foresters to look after the trees. Millions of rain forest trees are cut down every year, and very few are planted in their place. This is why the rain forests are in danger.

*Bundles of logs can be floated downstream to a sawmill.*

# At the sawmill

The logs are taken to a sawmill where the wood is cut into lumber that can then be sold.

When the logs arrive at the sawmill, they may be stored in water. This protects the logs and keeps them from drying out. Then they are fed into a machine that trims off the bark and cuts the logs into lumber. Different types of cuts can be used to show off the beautiful pattern, or **grain**, of the wood. The lumber is then stacked, graded, and sorted.

*Above* *Huge logs are cut into lumber at the sawmill.*

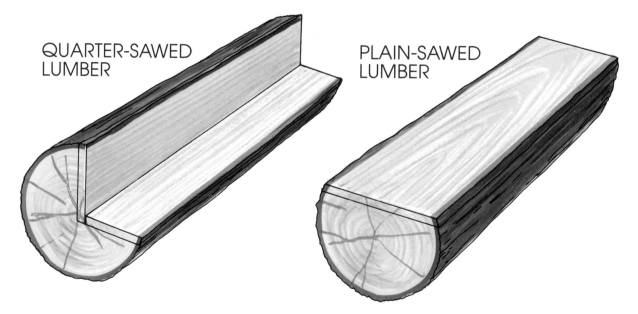

QUARTER-SAWED
LUMBER

PLAIN-SAWED
LUMBER

*Different ways of sawing logs to give an interesting grain.*

Freshly cut lumber cannot be used right away. This is because the wood is wet or still contains a lot of **sap**. This wood is called "green lumber." It usually has to be specially dried out before it can be used. Otherwise the wood shrinks, causing it to **warp** and crack.

The process of drying out is called seasoning. Seasoning can be done slowly in the open air or more quickly in a special type of warm oven called a **kiln**.

*Wood seasons slowly out in the open air.*

11

# Different kinds of wood

You can tell different kinds of wood from their grain. The grain is the pattern of tiny parallel lines you can see on a piece of wood. If the lines are close together, the wood is "close-grained." If they are wider apart, it is "open-grained."

Different types of wood are used for different jobs. Many softwoods, like pine and spruce, are open-grained. They are cheaper to buy and are more common than close-grained hardwoods. Softwoods are used to make everyday objects like kitchen furniture, shelves, and flooring.

*A close-up view of a hardwood and a softwood. What differences can you see?*

SOFTWOOD

pine

HARDWOOD

mahogany

| HARDWOODS | Typical appearance |
|---|---|
| Balsa: A lightweight wood that is used for insulation and model making. <br> Beech: Strong, easy to work with, and used for tools, furniture, gym equipment, and flooring. <br> Oak: Hard and strong and used for furniture, paneling, shipbuilding, and fences. <br> Teak: A hard-wearing wood used for furniture, chests and boxes, and shipbuilding. <br> Walnut: Polishes well and used for cabinetmaking, paneling, and furniture. |  |
| SOFTWOODS | |
| Cedar: Lightweight and used for paneling, fences, and roof coverings. <br> Cypress: Does not easily decay and used for flooring and building. <br> Larch: Strong and heavy and used for boat building and fences. <br> Pine: Easy to work with and carve and used for furniture, paneling, boxes, buildings, and fences. <br> Spruce: Easy to work with and used for ladders, oars, kitchen cabinets, musical instruments, and buildings. | |

Many hardwoods, like mahogany and ebony, are close-grained. Some hardwoods take hundreds of years to grow and are very expensive. They can be made into furniture that will last for many years. Furniture is also made from cheaper woods like pine, and is covered with a sheet of expensive wood called a veneer.

*Some common hardwood and softwood trees and their uses.*

13

# Wood as fuel

**Above** *A Lapp using wood as fuel.*

Wood is a very important **fuel**. More than half of the 3 billion tons of wood cut down each year is burned to light and heat people's homes.

If you use coal as a fuel in your home, you are still using wood. This is because coal is made from wood. Millions of years ago, tropical swamps and forests covered the earth. When the trees died, they fell into the swamps and were preserved. In time, the trees **fossilized** and turned into coal.

*Making charcoal in Brazil. The wood is burned under mounds of earth.*

Another type of fuel made from wood is charcoal. Charcoal is made by burning wood very slowly in ovens, under huge mounds of earth. You may have used charcoal at home on a barbecue grill.

Burning too much wood, coal, and oil as fuel may be harmful to our planet. When they are burned, they produce a gas called carbon dioxide. This is one of the gases in the **atmosphere** that traps heat from the sun. Producing too many of these gases means that too much heat is trapped in the atmosphere. This is sometimes called the "greenhouse effect."

*Burning wood, coal, or oil releases gases. These greenhouse gases may trap the sun's heat in the atmosphere, making our planet hotter.*

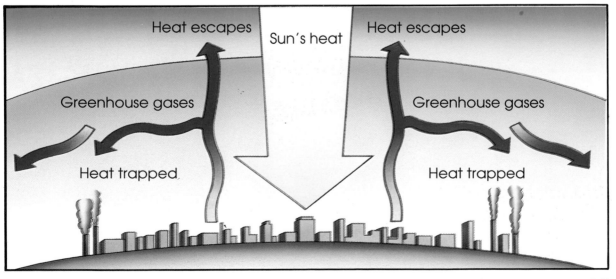

Heat escapes    Sun's heat    Heat escapes

Greenhouse gases    Greenhouse gases

Heat trapped    Heat trapped

# Using up waste wood

All wood is valuable. The smallest logs and even sawdust can be made into useful products.

Small logs are stripped and then chopped up into wood chips. The chips can be mixed with chemicals to make wood pulp. Wood pulp is used to make paper.

Blockboard is made up of blocks of wood that are glued together. These glued blocks are then sandwiched between thin sheets of veneer.

*This machine in Peru is used to make sheets of veneer for plywood.*

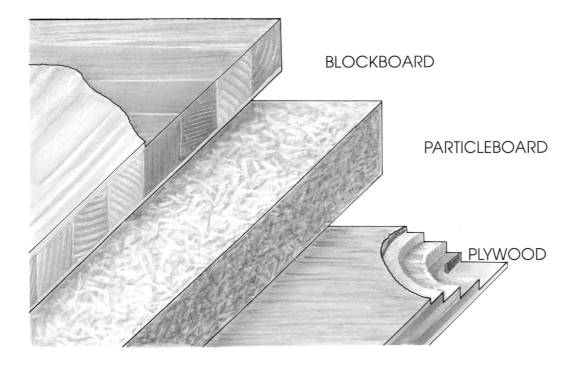

BLOCKBOARD

PARTICLEBOARD

PLYWOOD

Particleboard is made of wood chips and sawdust. They are mixed with a special glue, then pressed together very hard. When the glue dries, it makes a tough, strong material that can be used just like a piece of wood.

Plywood is a sandwich of thin sheets of wood or veneer glued together. The veneers are laid down so that the grain of each sheet of veneer lies in a different direction. This makes the material stronger and keeps it from warping. Plywood is useful in the building and furniture industries.

*Three ways that waste wood can be made into useful materials.*

# Chemicals from wood

Wood contains substances that can be separated out from the rest of the wood and made into chemicals.

Some pine trees contain resin from which other materials like **turpentine**, rosin, and chemicals are made. Violin players rub rosin on the bows of their violins because its stickiness helps to make a good sound. Gymnasts rub powdered rosin on their hands to help them grip the bars and ropes.

*Pine trees are cut to collect the sticky resin.*

*Creosote preserves wood so that it lasts for many years.*

Resin is also used in varnish, in paint, and in making paper.

By heating wood, other chemicals, such as tar, oil, wood alcohol (methylated spirit), and creosote, can be taken from it. The oil from wood is used to make **disinfectants**. Creosote can be painted on wood to preserve it. When the wood has been burned, charcoal and ash are left behind. Charcoal is a material that artists use for drawing. The ash is used as a **fertilizer**.

# Wood and paper

We would find it very difficult to live without paper and cardboard. Stores would not have paper bags or boxes, students would not have notebooks, and there would not be any books, newspapers, or magazines.

Most paper comes from softwood trees that have been grown especially for the paper industry. When the trees are cut down, they are turned into tiny wood chips. These chips are ground up and mixed with

*This diagram shows how wood chips are pulped and pressed to make paper that is then put on reels.*

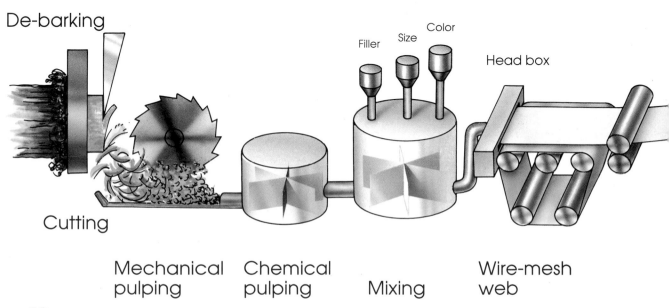

De-barking

Cutting

Filler

Size

Color

Head box

Mechanical pulping

Chemical pulping

Mixing

Wire-mesh web

chemicals to form a wet, sludgy wood pulp. The pulp contains lots of tiny wood **fibers**. These fibers are dried in thin sheets to form the paper. Some of the wood pulp used to make paper comes from waste wood from sawmills.

The wood pulp is fed into a machine that squeezes it between rollers to get rid of the water and press all the fibers together. As it passes through the rollers, the pulp gets drier and firmer. At the other end, it is ready to be wound into a huge roll of finished paper. Cardboard is made in the same way.

**Above** *Finished paper being wound onto enormous reels.*

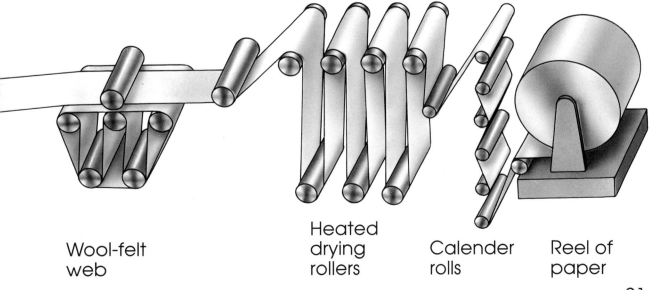

Wool-felt web

Heated drying rollers

Calender rolls

Reel of paper

# Building homes with wood

Wood is the oldest building material in the world, and it is still very popular today. Wood is easy to cut and use, and it is both strong and long lasting if it is taken care of properly.

In North America, the early pioneers built log cabins by laying logs one on top of another and filling the gaps with clay to keep out the wind and rain. This method of building used large amounts of **timber**.

**Above** *A traditional log house being built in Canada.*

**Right** *Siding being placed across the outside walls of a house.*

*The framework of a house is often made of wood.*

In Australia, Scandinavia, and in many parts of the United States, houses are built out of lumber. Large pieces of wood are used to build the frame of the house. This is then covered with wood siding. This wood is then coated with wood preservative, paint, or varnish to protect it from the weather.

Most houses that are built of other materials still have wood in them. They often have lumber framing, and flooring, doors, and window frames that are made of wood.

# Rain forests

Half the trees that grow on earth grow in the tropical rain forests. Rain forests grow in an area around the equator. They are needed for life on earth because they clean the air and help to control the world's climate. But the rain forests are in great danger.

*Cutting down the Brazilian rain forest. Once destroyed, the trees will not grow back again.*

Rain forest trees are being cut down but not replaced.

*A group of people in Australia trying to save the rain forests.*

Trees are sold for their valuable wood or are burned to clear land to grow crops or provide grazing for cattle. Many plants and animals in the rain forests die when the area is destroyed. And the land that is cleared for farming does not stay **fertile** for very long. With no trees to protect it, the land quickly becomes **barren** and the soil may be washed away.

Every five minutes about one square mile of rain forest is destroyed. If this keeps happening, all the rain forests will be gone in fifty years. People should know about the value of the rain forests and should **campaign** to save them.

*Unless we stop destroying the rain forest, much of it will be lost by the year 2000.*

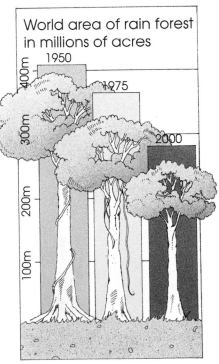

World area of rain forest in millions of acres
1950
1975
2000
400m
300m
200m
100m

# Recycling paper

Recycling paper can help to protect our forests. Although many softwood trees are grown to be used for paper and new trees are planted in their place, we could save trees and energy by recycling the ton of paper we throw away each year.

**Above** *Waste-paper arriving at a recycling plant.*

Wastepaper can easily be recycled to make good-quality new paper. The paper is put into a machine called a pulper. Here

*The paper to be recycled is pulped with hot water and chemicals.*

26

it is mixed with hot water and chemicals. The chemicals help to remove the ink, which would make the new paper look gray and dirty. Sometimes, the pulp is bleached to make it whiter. You can also recycle paper by simply pulping wastepaper with water.

*The pulp is finally turned into a roll of recycled paper.*

Experts think that we could keep around 35 million trees from being cut down each year if we recycled three-quarters of our paper and cardboard.

# Projects with wood

**Make a wooden boat**

You will need:

Wood scraps
A saw
Sandpaper
Glue

One or two corks
A matchstick
A paper flag
Waterproof paints and pens

1. Draw the outline of your boat on the wood. Ask an adult to help you cut it out with a saw. Sandpaper it carefully until it is smooth.

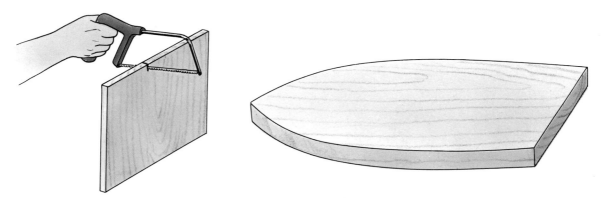

2. Glue the corks on to look like funnels. Glue your paper flag to the matchstick. Make a hole in one of the corks and push in the matchstick.

3. Decorate your boat with paints and pens. Varnish it to make it waterproof. Now you and your friends can have a race!

## Make a log cabin

You will need:

Sticks of wood
A craft knife
Glue

Gummed paper
Cardboard

1. With an adult to help you, cut half your sticks to about 5 inches in length, and the other half to about 2½ inches. Make a notch on either side of every stick, a little way in from each end.

2. Lay down two long sticks, one for the front and one for the back of the cabin, and glue them to your cardboard base. Lay two short sticks across the sides, gluing the notches together.

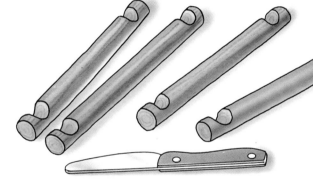

3. Keep building up the walls until they are as high as you want them to be. Glue the sticks together as you are building.

4. Cut out a rectangle of cardboard and bend it in the middle to make the roof. Cut out the shapes for the door and windows from gummed paper and stick them in place.

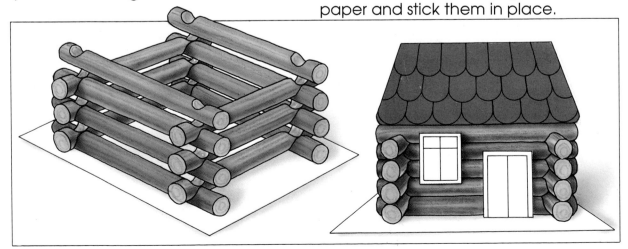

# Glossary

**Atmosphere**   The air that surrounds the earth.

**Barren**   A place is barren if plants and trees are not able to grow there.

**Campaign**   To take action for a purpose.

**Climate**   The usual weather of a particular place.

**Disinfectant**   A chemical substance that kills germs.

**Felled**   Cut or knocked down.

**Fertile**   Fertile land is rich and is good for growing crops.

**Fertilizer**   A substance that is spread on land to make plants grow better.

**Fiber**   A long thread, made of cells, found in trees and other plants.

**Fossilized**   When a plant (or animal) has been in the ground for millions of years and has become as hard as a rock.

**Fuel**   Anything that is burned to give off heat.

**Grain**   The pattern on wood made up by the fibers.

**Hardwood**   A type of tree with broad leaves. Most hardwoods are deciduous, which means they lose their leaves in autumn.

**Kiln**   An oven for drying wood.

**Logger**   A person who harvests trees.

**Nursery**   A place where trees are grown from seed.

**Recycling**   When materials that have been used before are treated so that they can be used again.

**Sap**   The juice, largely water, that flows through a plant.

**Sapling**   A young tree.

**Sawmill**   A place where trees are cut into lumber.

**Softwood**   A type of tree with thin, needlelike leaves that carries its seeds in cones. Most softwood trees are evergreen, which means they keep their leaves all year round.

**Timber**   Wood used for building.

**Tropical rain forest**   The thick forests found near the Equator, where the hot temperatures and heavy rainfall provide perfect conditions for trees and undergrowth to grow.

**Turpentine**   A kind of oil that comes from trees and can be used for cleaning paint brushes or thinning paint.

**Warp**   To bend. Wood warps if it is dried out too quickly.

# Books to read

Brown, William F. *Wood Works: Experiments with Common Wood and Tools*. New York: Macmillan, 1984.

Carrick, Graham. *Wood*. Vero Beach, Fla.: Rourke, 1990.

Dineen, Jacqueline. *Wood and Paper*. Hillside, NJ: Enslow, 1988.

Hamilton-MacLaren, Alistair. *Houses and Homes*. Technology Projects. New York: Bookwright, 1992.

Jennings, Terry. *Trees*. Junior Science. New York: Gloucester, 1991.

Whyman, Kathryn. *Structures and Materials*. Science Today. New York: Gloucester, 1987.

## Useful addresses

American Forest and Paper
  Association
260 Madison Avenue
New York, NY 10016

Forest Products Society
2801 Marshall Court
Madison, WI 53705

Greenpeace
1611 Connecticut Avenue
Washington, DC 20090

Society of Wood Science and
  Technology
One Gifford Pinchot Drive
Madison, WI 53705

# Index

## Picture acknowledgments

The publishers would like to thank the following for allowing their photographs to be reproduced in this book: J. Allan Cash Ltd, *cover* (top), 11; Bruce Coleman Ltd (John Anthony), 18; Environmental Picture Library, 26 (both), 27; Chris Fairclough Colour Library, *cover* (bottom), 19, 22 (top); Forestry Commission, 6, 8 (top); the Hutchison Library, 7 (top), 10; Marion Morrison, 16; Photri, 22 (bottom), 23; Tony Stone Worldwide, 5, 8 (bottom), 24; Wayland Picture Library, *title page*, 25; Zefa, 7 (bottom), 9, 14 (both), 21. Artwork by the Hayward Art Group, 13, 15; Janos Marffi, 4, 10, 12, 17, 20–21, 28–29, Elsa Godfrey, 25.